LOST LIVERIES OF PRIVATISATION
in Colour
For the Modeller and Historian

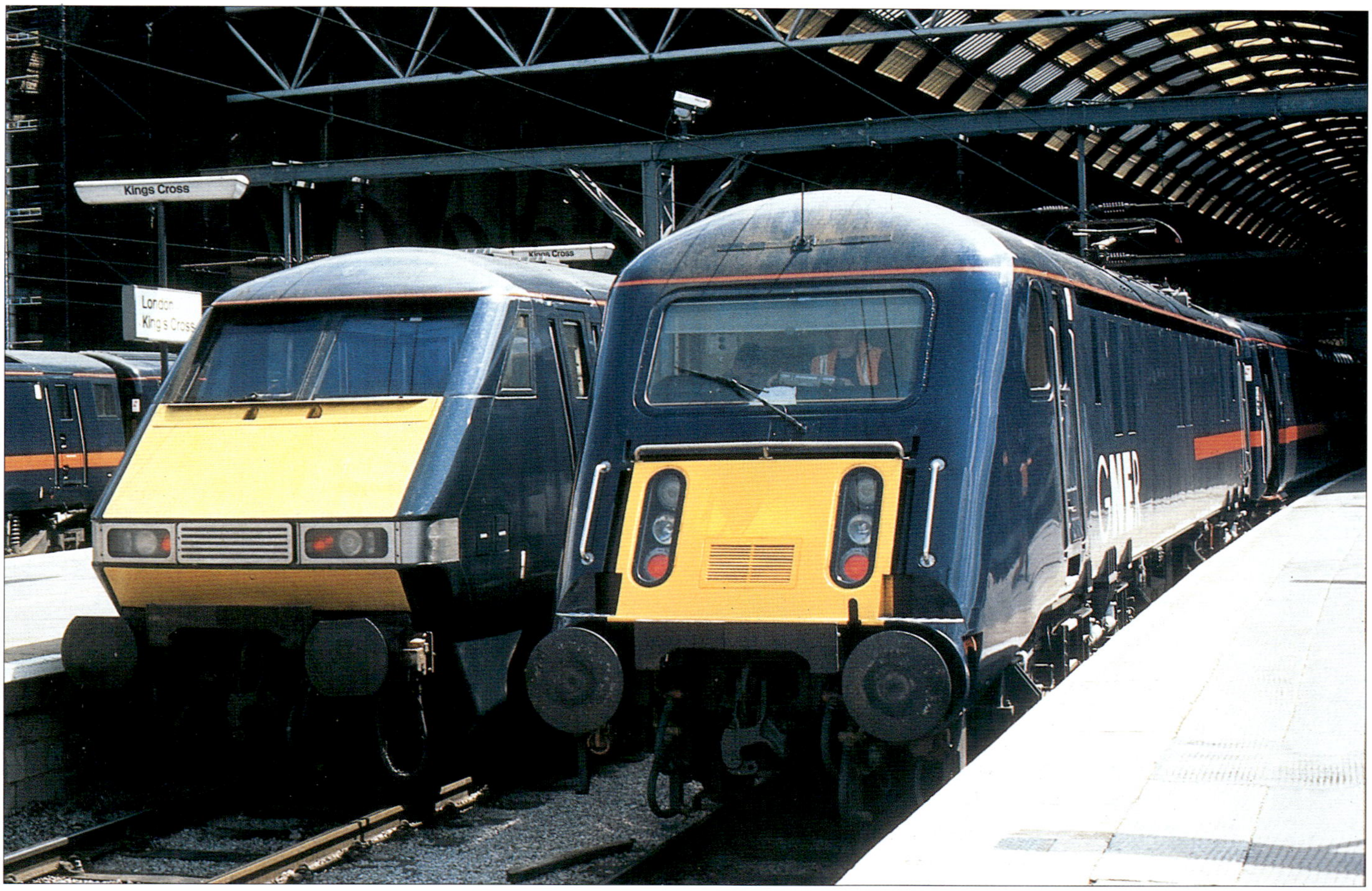

David Cable

First published 2009

ISBN 978 0 7110 3361 0

All rights reserved. No part of this book may be reproduced or transmitted in any form or by any means, electronic or mechanical, including photocopying, recording, scanning or by any information storage and retrieval system, on the internet or elsewhere, without permission from the Publisher in writing.

© David Cable 2009

Published by Ian Allan Publishing

an imprint of Ian Allan Publishing Ltd,
Hersham, Surrey KT12 4RG.
Printed in England by Ian Allan Printing Ltd,
Hersham, Surrey KT12 4RG.

Visit the Ian Allan Publishing website at
www.ianallanpublishing.com

Copyright
Illegal copying and selling of publications deprives authors, publishers and booksellers of income, without which there would be no investment in new publications. Unauthorised versions of publications are also likely to be inferior in quality and contain incorrect information. You can help by reporting copyright infringements and acts of piracy to the Publisher or the UK Copyright Service.

Title page: GNER Class 89 No 89 001 and a Class 91 stand side by side at King's Cross in July 1997.

CONTENTS

Introduction	3
Principles of a colour scheme	4
Advertising liveries	5
Pre-privatisation liveries	6
Passenger franchises	
Anglia	10
Cardiff Railway	13
Central	14
Chiltern	17
Cross-Country	18
Gatwick Express	20
Great Eastern	22
Great Western	26
InterCity East Coast	32
InterCity West Coast	36
Island Line	40
LTS Rail	40
Merseyrail Electrics	41
Midland Main Line	42
North London Railways	44
North West Regional Railways	46
Regional Railways North East	48
ScotRail	52
South Central	54
South Eastern	56
South Western	58
Thames	63
Thameslink	64
Wales & West	68
West Anglia Great Northern	75
Non-franchised passenger operations	
Eurostar	81
Heathrow Express	82
Hull Trains	84
Charter and spot-hire operators	
Cotswold Rail	85
Fragonset Railways / FM Rail	86
Victa Westlink Rail / Stobart Rail	88
Waterman Railways	89
Freight operators	
ARC	90
DRS	91
EWS	92
Foster Yeoman / Mendip Rail	94
Freightliner	96
GB Railfreight	97
National Power	97
Other organisations	
Adtranz	98
Bombardier	98
Hitachi	99
Hunslet Barclay	99
Porterbrook Leasing	100
Railtrack	102
Wessex Traincare	104

INTRODUCTION

It used to be said that if you had any spare cash you should invest it in companies that made white paint and cones for the roads. But since rail privatisation the prudent investor should perhaps have put his money into paint companies and those producing vinyl sheeting, such has been (and continues to be) the plethora of liveries and pictorial embellishments that have been dreamed up by the Train Operating Companies (TOCs) and other railway organisations.

To begin, it is worth recalling how basically simple things were in the last days of British Rail. Latterly there were five sectors – InterCity, Network SouthEast, Regional Railways, Rail Express Systems and Railfreight. Private companies included Freightliner, Foster Yeoman, ARC and National Power; in addition there were a number of smaller organisations, such as Hunslet Barclay, Waterman Railways and the seven PTEs. Although each of the five sectors had its own colour scheme, these were virtually universal across the network, whereas today, with the exception of the freight companies, particular colour schemes can normally be seen only on specific routes.

Considering the privatisation liveries that have now become (or are becoming) obsolete, we can say that there are a number of schemes which have worked very well, and, whilst not everyone will agree, the original Great Western Trains, Southern, GNER, Central Trains green, the Mendip Rail livery on No 59002 and the schemes used on the third-rail slam-door stock were, to me, simple and effective. It is interesting that two of these – GWT and Southern – reflected the pre-nationalisation companies, and it is perhaps unfortunate that the new franchise based on lines emanating from Euston and concentrated in the West Midlands, named London Midland, has chosen green rather than LMS crimson lake or even LNWR 'plum and spilt milk'!

Every time a franchise has changed hands a new colour scheme has been generated. Sometimes there has been an experimental livery, or labels have been affixed as an interim measure whilst the new scheme is being developed and then applied to the whole fleet. Inevitably, as with all occasions when liveries change, privatised locomotives and HST power cars would appear with InterCity and other liveried coaches and *vice versa*, but this was resolved in a surprisingly short time in comparison with the situation obtaining when, for example, BR's the InterCity and Network SouthEast identities were introduced. It is interesting that on the one hand, the only scheme that has survived from 1996 is the white Stagecoach livery used by South West Trains (although Chiltern's NSE-based scheme has scarcely changed either), whereas FirstGroup has applied three schemes since taking over the Great Western franchise, the cost of which has had to be borne by its customers.

Most of the new liveries were rushed into existence, although two operators in particular – LTS (with its rag-tag of units before the Class 357s) and Thames Trains – seemed to be in no hurry (although in the latter case this might have had something to do with NSE paint guarantees). And, indeed, the final trains on South Eastern lost Network SouthEast livery as recently as late 2007.

In addition to the many and varied paint schemes, a surprisingly large number of multiple-units have carried vinyl coverings depicting all sorts of messages. These have ranged from offering cheap fares, illustrating places on the line for a day out, special events, advertising products and companies, and promoting the Olympic bid to the extreme of graffiti (*why* did Virgin do this on a 'Pendolino'?). This has provided even more colour for those enthusiasts who enjoy the variety. But it is noteworthy that, contrasting with the situation in Germany, Austria and Switzerland, locomotives have seldom received non-standard colours, and the likes of Corus, Shanks, Bardon Hill, Medite, Malcolm Group, Stobart's 'Eddie the Engine', Teenage Spirit and Territorial Army 100 could surely open the way for more variations on the large number of standard Class 60s and 66s.

The situation is, of course, ever-changing, and by the time this publication is on sale it is likely that other liveries will have disappeared. It is interesting to note how few locomotives have been involved compared with the number of multiple-units and single railcars. Only four franchises have seen locomotive liveries entirely 'lost', these being Great Western (GWT green), Anglia (turquoise), InterCity West Coast (Virgin Trains red and grey) and InterCity East Coast (GNER blue); however, South West Trains' Class 73s have had their liveries modified, as have the Class 20s, 37s and 47s of freight operator DRS, and GB Railfreight's Class 66s are probably in line for similar treatment.

This book concentrates on the colour schemes that have been applied to the main-line rolling stock of the major TOCs since privatisation in 1996 up to the granting of new franchises in late 2007 (and their adoption during 2008) but which have now disappeared or are expected to do so in the near future. It also covers the majority of the advertising schemes used on the TOC trains, as well as the rolling stock used for regular main-line support activities and a selection of depot shunters. A few photographs of the pre-1996 schemes are also included, to remind readers of liveries that were lost as a result of privatisation. As the PTEs were not affected by privatisation they have not been included in this book; a forthcoming companion volume on the passenger sectors will cover all their variations. However, two schemes have been modified since privatisation, and for the sake of completeness these changes are shown.

It is not the intention to show every temporary or small detail variation, such as a new franchise-holder's name on the previous operator's colours, or, indeed, every permutation of a basic colour scheme, such as that of the FirstGroup. Similarly, space considerations have precluded the depiction of every promotional livery, and those that are shown are intended to be a representative selection.

As always, Peter Waller and his colleagues at Ian Allan Publishing have been of great help in getting this book into print, and I appreciate all their efforts. Photographs are from my own collection except where credited to others, and to those persons I extend my thanks for their help.

With a publication such as this it is impossible to keep up with changes, particularly with regard to advertising liveries, so a cut-off date has been set as December 2008. It is, therefore, entirely probable that by the time this book appears in print further changes will have occurred, resulting in the loss of yet more liveries. Such is progress!

David Cable
Hartley Wintney
January 2009

PRINCIPLES OF COLOUR SCHEME

Above: The early 'EW&S' branding is seen on Class 37/4 No 37415 and an inspection saloon as they trundle past Manor Farm, Cholsey, in March 1997. EWS colours are shown in more detail on page 92.

Beauty is in the eye of the beholder. The main BR schemes of green for locomotives and maroon for coaches or blue for locomotives and blue-and-grey for coaches were effective in presenting a product, the straight lines and simplicity of which gave an impression of length and therefore sleekness and speed. And BR learned lessons, such as the improvement that resulted from abandoning the original NSE scheme for locomotives with swept-up ends in favour of the straight bands to emphasise length. But to the author, some of the schemes dreamed up for the privatised companies can only be described as messy, if not revolting. It may be appropriate to consider, therefore, what basic principles a livery design should endeavour to follow. Applicable to schemes that have disappeared and to those that remain extant, the comments that follow are subjective but have been endorsed by Mike Denny of the Roundel Design Group.

A livery should identify the product or owner and be fit for purpose. In this respect it should follow certain principles, viz:

- It must reflect the size and shape of the object being used, and the agreed livery must respect the form of the item. In this regard, the schemes applied by Stagecoach to its electric multiple-units and by Virgin to its 'Pendolinos' and 'Voyagers' are fine when applied to a full-length train but look too compacted on single-car units, Class 73s and Class 57s.

- The colours should harmonise. Alphaline, Connex yellow and white and locomotive-hauled Virgin trains do not offend, whereas ScotRail looks as if the paintbox has been raided, and the red, orange and yellow swirls on the SWT Class 450s just clash with the royal-blue bodies. The red scheme used with SWT Class 455s looks cheap in comparison with BR maroon or LMS crimson lake. But 'heritage' colours do not work on modern vehicles.

- It should be fairly simple and should try to convey a meaning or background. Schemes used for a bus may be quite wrong for a train, and the bus companies that have taken on train operations have generally failed to recognise this. FirstGroup trains with meaningless squiggles and blocks of small lines on a purple background look, frankly, awful (although the IC125 power cars in plain colours appear quite smart). And as for the two Class 319s in rainbow colours with pink ends …

- The colours should avoid (or at least minimise) showing up blemishes such as oil spillages, brake dust and effects of the weather. They should still look good after several years of wear, tear and washing in chemicals.

- The need for visually impaired persons easily to locate the doors should be incorporated sensibly. The schemes used by Southern and c2c and the grey-and-blue livery on Silverlink's Class 350s blend well with other colours of the train whilst still giving door prominence, and Thames Trains' green motifs around the door areas have been effective. On Stagecoach's white express units the orange single doors, picking out one of the front-end 'swirl' colours, look fine, but on blue Class 450s and red Class 455s, with their double doors, the result is, to say the least, garish.

- If trains in a franchise are going to be painted in different colours to identify different types of units for different services, those trains should be kept to their correct duties. The use of blue outer-suburban Class 450s on Portsmouth express duties does not convey an image of an express service.

ADVERTISING LIVERIES

This book describes all advertising liveries which had been eliminated by the end of 2008. However, some liveries had been introduced before that date but were still in existance after that time. Although not exhaustive, due to the pace of change, the following list gives an indication of some non-standard colour schemes that can still be seen but which are not portrayed, being outside the scope of this book.

121020	Chiltern blue	156484	Settle & Carlisle line
150271	Rugby League (Northern Rail Cup)	158787/92-6	Sheffield–Leeds fast service
150272	R&B Festival, Colne	170420	Glasgow 2014
153329	St Ives Bay Partnership	319364/5	Thameslink rainbow and pink
153369	Looe Valley line	357010	c2c green train
155341-7	Calder Valley line	375610	Royal Tunbridge Wells
156402	Chapelfield Shopping Centre	456006	Transport for London Security
156461	Ravenglass & Eskdale Railway	Class 460	Fly Emirates
156469	Sheffield–Leeds fast service		

Below: Anglia Railways, Class 86 No 86 219 *NHS 50* at Liverpool Street in July 1998, having arrived with an express from Norwich.

for the Modeller and Historian

PRE-PRIVATISATION LIVERIES

Left: The final version of InterCity livery is displayed on Class 47/4 No 47810, bringing a diverted Manchester–Brighton express through Dorking West in June 1993.

Below left: For a short period Class 50s worked with '4-TC' sets on the Salisbury services. In this view Network SouthEast-liveried Class 50 No 50030 *Repulse* draws into Grateley station with a train for Waterloo in August 1989.

Bottom: The standard Regional Railways colours gleam in the sun as Class 37/4 No 37421 *The Kingsman* heads its Crewe–Holyhead train past Rowton, near Chester, in June 1994.

Right: The Class 158 'Express' DMUs were painted in a different scheme from other Regional Railways units. Here No 158713 leaves Gleneagles as it heads south on its way from Aberdeen to Glasgow in May 1991.

Below right: The rich red of Rail Express Systems is shown off here by Class 47/4 No 47630 speeding past Hugus in April 1992 with a Penzance–Leeds parcels service. Note the raised BR double-arrow symbol. In terms of livery the train was particularly varied, comprising a mix of plain BR blue, blue and grey, InterCity and Post Office red and yellow – a worthy subject for the modeller!

LOST LIVERIES OF PRIVATISATION in colour

for the Modeller and Historian

7

LOST LIVERIES OF PRIVATISATION in colour

Left: A less-than-common shot of a Class 37 on the South Western main line to Exeter. Having arrived from the Yeovil direction, Class 37 No 37012, in 'Dutch' grey and yellow, pauses with an inspection saloon at Templecombe before returning whence it came. The station's award-winning cleanliness is readily apparent in this photograph, taken in June 1992.

Left: Although a pre-privatisation livery this was very much a non-standard scheme. The Railway Technical Centre colours of red and grey are shown to good advantage as Class 47/4 No 47972 *The Royal Army Ordnance Corps* brings a southbound test train past Carpenders Park in March 1993. This scheme lasted well into the privatisation era. Note the variety of coaching stock.

Top: With prominent Transrail logos superimposed on its existing Trainload Freight livery, Class 60 No 60058 *John Howard* leaves Runcorn behind in May 1995 as it passes Daresbury with the Stanlow–Jarrow tanks, a traffic since lost to the railway.

Above right: In Loadhaul black and orange, with prominent 'Loadhaul' logo, Class 37/7 No 37710 heads north through Monk Fryston in July 1996 with a Wakefield–Lackenby steel train.

Right: The last days of the Willesden Railnet–Dover Royal Mail service. In Mainline blue, Class 73/1 No 73133 *The Bluebell Railway* takes the Redhill line at Coulsdon in July 2003, with No 73136 *Kent Youth Music* bringing up the rear. The former displays a number of detail variations from standard, notably revised light clusters and the removal from behind the centre cab window of the Southern Region two-character headcode display.

for the Modeller and Historian

PASSENGER FRANCHISES

Anglia Railways (Anglia / ONE Anglia / National Express East Anglia)

10   LOST LIVERIES OF PRIVATISATION in colour

Above left: Anglia livery as applied to locomotives and Class 153 and 156 DMUs, consisting of turquoise with white stripes and 'Anglia' in white script, and with the locomotive/unit number on the front end rather than the cab side. In November 2003 a complete Anglia-liveried Norwich–Liverpool Street express is brought into Ipswich station by Class 86/2 No 86215 *The Round Tabler*; note the 'Anglia' name repeated in the locomotive's centre cab window. In 2002 similar No 86227 was decked out with a large Union Jack on each side to celebrate HM The Queen's Golden Jubilee.

Left: One of the DMU versions of Anglia livery is seen in winter light (hence the shadows) as Class 150 'Sprinter' No 150227 leaves Ipswich for Lowestoft in November 2003.

Above: Anglia livery as applied to Class 170 DMUs, comprising turquoise lower bodysides, with white upper bodyside and black windows, 'Anglia' being superimposed in white on the turquoise lower bodyside. Occasional trains between London and Norwich were worked by these units; here No 170207 brings up the rear of a Norwich–Liverpool Street service passing Stratford in February 2000. The low sun highlights the colours very well.

Right: The new livery devised by National Express for the Anglia franchise consisted of a light-grey bodyside with dark-grey ventilation louvres and multi-coloured stripes around cab sides, 'one' (in all-lower-case lettering) and 'Anglia' appearing in white on the lower bodysides. Here Class 47/4 No 47818 brings a pair of debranded coaches along the down fast line at Romford in January 2008.

Top: As originally repainted, two Class 90 locomotives, Nos 90003 and 90004, had dark-grey bodysides. Here No 90004 speeds through Shenfield with a Liverpool Street–Norwich express in June 2004. This locomotive would later be repainted in standard grey.

Above: Halfway house. Still in grey but having lost its earlier markings and stripes, Class 90 No 90010 arrives at Colchester with a Norwich–Liverpool Street express in April 2008. Showing off an intermediate livery pending the application of the new National Express colours, the locomotive now has a white lower-bodyside stripe embellished with 'national express East Anglia'. Note that the uniformity of the train is broken by the third coach, already in full NXEA livery.

Right: Livery promoting the Norfolk & Norwich Festival. With precisely 2 minutes and 31 seconds to go before departure for Peterborough, Class 153 DMU No 153314 stands at Ipswich in November 2003. The dates on the bodyside reveal that the decals are long overdue for replacement.

Cardiff Railway (Valley Lines)

Above: A match at Cardiff National Stadium means augmented trains are required on the Radyr–Cardiff services. In standard Valley Lines livery of red, white and green, Class 142 'Pacer' unit No 142076 leads similar No 142080 on one such service at Caerphilly in February 2003.

Left: About to depart Radyr station for Cardiff in February 2000, Class 143 unit No 143611 shows off its experimental Valley Lines promotional livery, comprising a light-blue lower body, orange window frames and yellow and green bands. Is the guard Harry Worth?

Below: The Class 150s used in the Welsh Valleys and on services such as this Aberdare–Barry Island working displayed advertising on their two differently coloured coaches. No 150280 arrives at Taffs Well in February 2003.

for the Modeller and Historian

Central Trains

Above: Central Trains' livery consisted of two-tone green with blue cab-window surrounds and yellow doors, 'Central' appearing on the bodyside along with (as originally devised) telephone number 0800 00 60 60. The livery sits nicely on Class 156 'Super Sprinter' No 156401 as it waits to leave Skegness for Crewe in September 2004, although passengers seem to be in the minority!

Left: The final version of Central Trains livery – turquoise with white lower-bodyside band, dark-grey roof, pale-blue doors and three white semi-circles around the cab doors. Class 170 No 170112 passes Undy on its way from Cardiff to Nottingham in September 2005.

Above right: This somewhat overwhelming pink scheme was applied to Class 170 No 170399 to promote Birmingham's claim to be European City of Culture in 2008. Forming a Birmingham–Liverpool service, the unit is seen speeding north past Slindon in August 2003. *Howard Osiraaski*

Right: No 170513 was decorated in 'Robin Hood Line' colours to celebrate the reopening of the line from Nottingham through Mansfield. The unit is seen in May 2003 passing the remains of the old branch to Hereford at Grange Court while *en route* from Nottingham to Cardiff.

for the Modeller and Historian 15

Above: Another promotional livery worn by a Central Trains Class 170 was this striking scheme to the order of Birmingham's Bull Ring Centre. The tide is out as No 170505, on a Nottingham–Cardiff service, passes the River Severn at Purton in September 2003.

Below: Yet more Central Trains advertising, this time for the Derwent Valley Mills Partnership, was applied to No 170399, seen passing Churchdown while *en route* from Gloucester to Nottingham in August 2004.

Chiltern (Chiltern Railways)

Above: When the Chiltern franchise was awarded, the Class 165 units were still quite new and thus retained their existing NSE livery for several years. This post-privatisation scene features No 165006 leaving Denham Golf Club, with its old GWR pagoda, on an all-stations service from Aylesbury to Marylebone in June 1999. In common with the newer Class 168s the '165s' are now in Chiltern's new colours, which are very similar to those seen here.

Below: No 165037 arrives at Denham with a train from High Wycombe to Marylebone in March 2005.

for the Modeller and Historian

Cross-Country
(Virgin CrossCountry)

Above: Virgin Trains livery as applied to HST sets used on CrossCountry services, with an 'XC' device (soon deleted) in addition to the standard 'Virgin' script. Buffer-fitted power car No 43068 *The Red Nose* brings up the rear of a Bournemouth–Manchester express at Basingstoke in September 1997. Note that on the power car the charcoal grey is restricted to the guard's-compartment end.

Left: Displaying the standard Virgin livery as applied to locomotives, comprising a red bodyside with charcoal-grey cabsides and three low-level white stripes, Class 47/4 No 47817 *The Institution of Mechanical Engineers* hurtles through Bramley with an Edinburgh–Bournemouth express one afternoon in July 2001.

LOST LIVERIES OF PRIVATISATION in colour

Above: The silver livery as applied to Virgin's 'Voyager' units will endure on the West Coast route, but the CrossCountry version, with 'crosscountry' 'XC' logos in red and white, became obsolete upon Arriva's takeover of the franchise. Passing Purley-on-Thames on a Birmingham–Reading service in April 2008, an unidentified Class 220 shows off the interim scheme, before the application of the brown nose. Note the yellow cantrail band, the yellow element of the coupling gear and the labels in the windows to indicate the First-class area.

Below: Shadows from the low winter sun block out the running gear of HST power car No 43101, but the sun highlights the logo promoting the 'Irish Mail', in both English and Welsh, together with a shamrock. The train is a Bournemouth–Manchester service, photographed at Reading in February 1999.

for the Modeller and Historian

19

Gatwick Express

Left: The revised Gatwick Express livery was similar to the BR's InterCity scheme which it replaced but featured a maroon band in lieu of red, and with 'Gatwick Express' and two flashes in grey on the upper bodyside. Passing South Croydon in August 2000, Class 73/2 No 73207 and its matching Driving Luggage Van contrast with the Mk 2 coaching stock embellished with blue advertising to the order of Continental Airlines.

Below: The striking livery applied to the Class 460 'Juniper' units – white with blue lower-bodyside band, with red around the (yellow) front end and along the roof, grey doors and 'express' in grey on the lower bodyside and Gatwick Express in white on the roof of the power cars.
No 460006 works a Victoria–Gatwick Airport service through Wandsworth Common in August 2004.

Left: 'Juniper' No 460003 shows off its Continental Airlines advertising livery as it passes Salfords en route to Victoria in September 2005. Originally white, the set number (03) now appears in black for easier visibility.

LOST LIVERIES OF PRIVATISATION in colour

Above: Advertising for Continental Airlines gave way to that for Delta Airlines. No 460008 keeps to the 40mph limit as it passes Earlswood on its way to Gatwick Airport in January 2007.

Below: Another airline promoted by Gatwick Express was Emirates. With gold-painted doors and triangular motifs between coaches, No 460004 shows off the interim version, as it heads north through Clapham Junction in December 2008.

Great Eastern Railway (Great Eastern Trains / First Great Eastern / ONE Great Eastern)

Above: On loan to Silverlink following the accident near Watford Junction, Great Eastern Trains No 321446 enters Euston on a service from Milton Keynes in July 1998. The unit is in basic Great Eastern Trains livery, but any indication of its regular operator has been removed, along with the FirstGroup logo.

Left: With Great Eastern and First logos on bodysides and front ends, First Great Eastern Class 312/0 EMU No 312703 leaves Colchester in June 2003 on a stopping service for Walton-on-the Naze.

Below left: First Great Eastern's Class 360 EMUs were delivered in FirstGroup purple, pink and white, with 'First' on the ends and centrally on the bodysides and 'Great Eastern' on the bodysides only. Seen on its delivery run in a DB transfer freight from Eifeltor to Nippes yards, No 360111 passes Köln West in June 2003.

Top right: Along with the pink stripes, all lettering was removed from the Great Eastern Class 360s following the transfer of the franchise to National Express. In plain purple with white doors and devoid of any identification, No 360104 departs Colchester for Harwich in February 2008.

Right: Following refurbishment Great Eastern Class 315 units appeared in plain purple with white doors. No 315806 shows off this livery as it speeds past Pudding Mill Lane on its way to Shenfield in June 2006.

for the Modeller and Historian

23

Left: Tailing a similar unit still in Great Eastern Trains livery, Class 321 No 321446 shows off the Great Eastern version of ONE colours. Photographed in September 2004, the pair are forming a Southend–Liverpool Street service, seen passing Pudding Mill Lane as a DLR train to Stratford approaches (left).

Centre left: Snapped under the fluorescent lights of Liverpool Street, Class 321 No 321330 shows off its Braintree Free Port advertising livery in September 2000.

Bottom left: Seen on a Liverpool Street–Braintree service, Class 321 No 321308, in 3M advertising livery, passes the new platform at Stratford in August 1996. Note that the driving trailers are white and grey with 3M logos in red, while the other coaches feature illustrations of group products.

Right: The intermediate coaches of No 321308, seen in close-up at Liverpool Street.

Below: A short-lived promotional livery was this East of England scheme intended to encourage investment in East Anglia. The pale yellow/green catches the sun at Pudding Mill Lane as unit No 321366 heads for Southend in November 2002.

for the Modeller and Historian

Great Western (Great Western Trains / First Great Western)

Above: Great Western Trains adopted a livery of dark green and white with a stone-coloured strip at the base of the bodyside, while the words 'Great Western', in white, were accompanied on the green area of HST power cars by a stylised osprey motif within an oval surround, the motif being reversed on the carriage sides. Diverted via Gloucester as a result of closure of the Severn Tunnel, a Paddington–Swansea express headed by No 43010 approaches Standish Junction in May 1999.

Left: The race is on at Lower Basildon in May 1999 as an up Swansea HST pulls ahead of an up Worcester HST headed by power car No 43036, the latter being speed-restricted on the up relief line.

Above right: Great Western Trains' osprey logo and style of lettering are shown to good advantage on HST power car No 43183 at Reading in October 1996.

Right: Class 47 locomotives operated by Great Western trains were given a livery of plain dark green with white lettering and osprey logo on the bodyside at No 1 end. Representing this scheme is Class 47/4 No 47815, passing Shottesbrooke with a train of racegoers from Paddington to Cheltenham in March 1999.

for the Modeller and Historian

Left: FirstGroup revised the original Great Western livery, introducing a gold band and gold 'First' logo and adding thin green lines to the white areas to give shading effect. The effect is shown well in this view of HST power car No 43106 at the rear of a Penzance–Paddington service rounding the bend at Crofton in August 1999.

Below: Three livery variations are in evidence in this photograph, taken at Cholsey in November 1999. In plain green with gold First logo, Class 47/4 No 47846 *Thor* heads an empty HST set, of which the leading power car is in the original Great Western Trains scheme, the remainder in First Great Western green, white and gold.

Right: In First Great Western locomotive livery of green with a gold band and 'First' logo, Class 47/4 No 47811 backs the stock of a Penzance-bound motor-rail service into Paddington's Platform 1 in August 2000. Note the motor-rail van in matching colours.

Below right: Frustrating at the time, but worthwhile in retrospect: the subject of this photograph, taken near South Stoke in April 2002, was intended to be Class 57/6 No 57601, but it turned up double-headed by '47/4' No 47830. The train is the morning Plymouth–Bristol–Paddington express.

for the Modeller and Historian

29

LOST LIVERIES OF PRIVATISATION in colour

Above left: Eventually FirstGroup's house colours replaced Great Western green. For a short period the HST power cars had white colouring around the cab area, an example being No 43012, seen at Cholsey in December 2001 *en route* from Bristol to Paddington.

Left: In a different form, white embellishments were used on the Class 180 'Adelante' DMUs. No 180111 is seen passing Denchworth at full line speed on its way from Paddington to Cardiff in August 2002.

Above: Later repaints of HST power cars omitted the white window surrounds. Diverted over the old LSWR route as a result of engineering works on the Great Western line east of Reading, No 43026 is seen just west of Bracknell on a London-bound working in August 2003.

Right: Only two power cars were finished off with the 'dynamic lines' swirls used on FGW coaches, and these soon lost this effect, thereby adopting the current standard plain blue. In this view, recorded in August 2006, No 43009 brings a Bristol–Paddington express along the up relief line at Lower Basildon.

for the Modeller and Historian 31

InterCity East Coast (Great North Eastern Railway / National Express East Coast)

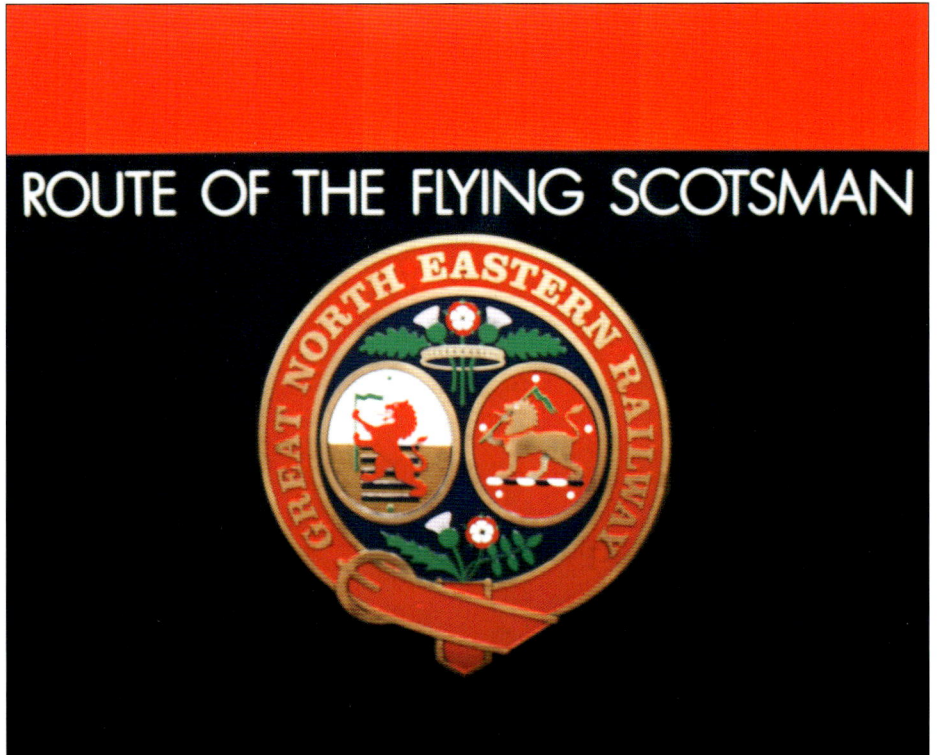

Above: Great North Eastern Railway adopted an attractive livery of dark blue with a red band and 'GNER' branding in gold. Class 91 No 91111 *Terence Cuneo* very conveniently came to a halt at Alexandra Palace in March 2004 whilst working a King's Cross–Leeds express. Note the orange doors of the Mk 4 coaches, this being a later addition to aid the partially sighted.

Left: Close-up of the bodyside crest applied to GNER coaching stock, along with reference to the 'Flying Scotsman'.

Above right: In a short-lived version of GNER livery, with the logo in white rather than gold, unique Class 89 locomotive No 89001 propels its Bradford–King's Cross express past Alexandra Palace in October 1997.

Right: To bolster services on the East Coast main line GNER borrowed Class 373 sets surplus to the requirements of Eurostar. The low sun highlights set No 3305, in full GNER livery, bringing up the rear of a Leeds–King's Cross express at Alexandra Palace in November 2005. Note that the power car, bearing the name *Yorkshire Forward*, has the GNER logo in gold but lacks a red stripe, presumably on account of the grille which dominates the bodyside.

32   LOST LIVERIES OF PRIVATISATION in colour

for the Modeller and Historian

Above: Unique to Class 90 No 90024 was this livery of dark blue with red stripe but no franchise identification. Propelling a full set of Anglia-liveried coaching stock forming a late-morning Liverpool Street–Norwich express, the locomotive is seen passing Pudding Mill Lane in April 2004.

Below: To help promote London's Olympic bid power cars Nos 43116 and 43120 had the words 'LONDON 2012 CANDIDATE CITY' emblazoned in white on the bodyside. This photograph was taken at King's Cross on the occasion of the unveiling ceremony on 18 February 2005. *Brian Morrison*

Right: Representing the interim situation on the East Coast main line, power car No 43316 heads an Aberdeen–King's Cross HST through Brookmans Park in February 2008. Livery is GNER dark blue with logo removed and red band replaced by one in National Express white; note, however, that the coaches retain their red doors.

Below: Prior to the transfer of the franchise a number of HST power cars had promotional decals affixed to otherwise standard GNER livery. Among these was No 43290, used to promote an enhanced service between London and Leeds, but when photographed at King's Cross in August 2007 it had just arrived with an express from Aberdeen, for which the lettering was somewhat inappropriate.

for the Modeller and Historian 35

InterCity West Coast (Virgin Trains)

36   LOST LIVERIES OF PRIVATISATION in colour

Left: In standard Virgin Trains livery of red with charcoal-grey cabs and three white bodyside stripes, Class 87 No 87029 *Earl Marischal* propels a Liverpool–Euston express past South Kenton in September 2003. Note that, unusually, an additional DVT is marshalled between the locomotive and coaches.

Below left: For a brief period Class 86/2 No 86245 *Caledonian* wore a variation of Virgin livery with Caledonian blue in place of red, and maroon stripes in lieu of white, being seen thus departing Euston with an express for Birmingham in July 1998. Note the absence of any operator identification.

Right: Class 08 No 08934, the Willesden shunter, was painted black with a chequered flag. The buddleia bush opposite the depot has intruded slightly in this photograph, taken in August 2000 from a Bakerloo Line train bound for Elephant & Castle.

Below: To encourage passengers to use its restaurant facilities Virgin applied 'Big Dish' promotional decals to Class 90 No 90014. Otherwise in standard livery, the locomotive is seen propelling a Glasgow–Euston express past Carpenders Park in February 1999.

for the Modeller and Historian

Below: Class 87 No 87012 *Cœur de Lion* was selected to help publicise London's campaign to stage the 2012 Olympics. Curiously the livery chosen was that of Network SouthEast – long since obsolete, and never previously applied to a Class 87. In July 2005 the locomotive was photographed passing Headstone Lane with a special that had started from Victoria behind GB Railfreight Class 66/7 No 66715 (just visible at the rear) and would continue via Bescot as far as Crewe before returning to the capital, terminating at Euston.

Left: In March 2005 Class 87 No 87019 was given a pseudo-LNWR livery of black with red and white lining and named *ACoRP – Association of Community Rail Partnerships*. Looking very smart, the locomotive is seen passing South Kenton in May 2006 with four Class 325 units on their way from Wembley Railnet to Shieldmuir. Fortunately for the photographer the Bakerloo Line train got out of the way just in time!

Top right: Although the livery applied to Virgin's 'Pendolino' fleet remains current, one of these units has been decorated in two non-standard schemes. Adorned with vinyls publicising the film *Spiderman*, No 390029 passes Rugby on a Manchester–Euston service in October 2006.

Right: The second non-standard livery (if such a word can be used to describe it) applied to No 390029 was this 'Graffiti' scheme. Here, passing Kenton on a Manchester–Euston service, the 'Pendolino' contrasts with a Harrow & Wealdstone Bakerloo Line train in a more practical and dignified colour scheme. The photograph was taken in July 2007.

38   LOST LIVERIES OF PRIVATISATION in colour

for the Modeller and Historian 39

Island Line

Above: Island Line's ex-London Underground Class 483 EMUs were painted in a promotional livery consisting of a light-blue background with multi-coloured dinosaurs etc in yellow, green, red and white. Here the tide is in and the Ryde skyline towers over No 483006 as it leaves Ryde Pier Head on its way to Shanklin in June 2000.

LTS Rail (LTS / c2c)

Below: The original scheme devised for the LTS line's Class 357s was this rather tasteful white and green livery, seen on No 357028 as it passes West Ham on a Fenchurch Street–Shoeburyness service in August 2000.

Right: The Class 357/2 units originally had this less attractive, simpler scheme, before all Class 357s were reliveried in c2c colours. No 357205 passes Shadwell on its way to Shoeburyness in January 2002.

Merseyrail Electrics

Right: Under the pre-privatisation regime of Regional Railways Merseyrail had already introduced its own livery of yellow, white, grey and black, these colours being retained by Arriva until reallocation of the franchise to Serco/Ned Railways. This photograph shows Class 507 EMU No 507021 leaving Sandhills on a Hunts Cross–Southport service in May 1993.

Midland Main Line (Midland Mainline)

Left: Midland Mainline adopted a livery of bluish green and white with orange stripes and a white motif resembling a prancing deer. Not long out of the paint shop, HST power car No 43049 brings up the rear of a Sheffield–St Pancras express passing Wellingborough in March 1997.

Below left: St Pancras as it used to be, with Class 170 DMU No 170106 waiting to depart for Nottingham in June 1999.

Right: Helping out the Midland main line whilst engineering work was affecting the LNW route into Manchester, debranded Virgin power car No 43104, still in red and charcoal but devoid of any identification, heads a mixed rake of HST stock passing Luton Airport Parkway on an express from Leeds in December 2002.

Below right: For its HST units Midland Mainline later adopted this attractive livery of blue, dark grey and white with an orange stripe at solebar level. Doing somewhat more than the 40mph suggested by the sign, No 43079 speeds past Harrowden Junction on a Manchester–St Pancras service in April 2004.

Below: A similar scheme was applied to the new Class 222 'Meridian' units. In this view the mist has almost cleared as No 222013 passes Wellingborough *en route* from Nottingham to St Pancras in March 2007.

for the Modeller and Historian 43

North London Railways (Silverlink)

Above: Silverlink on parade at Kenton in July 2007, as Class 321 EMU No 321426 from Milton Keynes overtakes Class 313 No 313105 from Watford Junction as they both make their way to Euston. The '313s' were given 'Silverlink City' branding, whereas the '321s' (and Class 150 DMUs) were labelled 'Silverlink County'.

Left: On the same day Siemens Class 350 No 350128, in the interim livery of grey and blue, heads north on a late-afternoon commuter service to Northampton.

Below: At least one Class 350 gained a variation of the interim scheme, No 350118 being devoid of the blue window surrounds as it passes Carpenders Park on its way up to Euston in July 2008.

Above: Unit No 321428 was chosen to advertise the new franchise for Silverlink, and appeared in three different colour schemes. In plain white with the words 'make the link', it is seen passing Carpenders Park on a Euston–Birmingham service in April 1998.

Below: No 321428 next appeared in the livery advertising a £7 fare from London to Birmingham, being seen thus about to leave Euston for Milton Keynes in July 1998.

Bottom: The final advertising scheme applied to No 321428 was this silver, green and blue version, caught by the low autumn sun at Headstone Lane in November 1999 as the unit was travelling from Birmingham to Euston on the up slow line.

North West Regional Railways (North Western Trains / First North Western)

Above: In North Western Trains blue with large gold stars and the operator's name in white, former Stansted Express Class 322 EMU No 322484 passes Headstone Lane in August 1998 on the unsuccessful service from Manchester Airport to Euston.

Left: FirstGroup has now taken over the North West franchise, as evident on Class 150/1 'Sprinter' DMU No 150139 as it leaves the through lines at Manchester Piccadilly on its way to Windermere in June 2000.

Above right: Back to its original haunts, working a Stansted Express service, Class 322 No 322484 had lost all North West Trains identification by the time it was photographed standing forlornly at Liverpool Street in October 1999.

Right: In newly applied Manchester Airport livery, Regional Railways' Class 309 No 309624 arrives at Manchester Airport station on 21 May 1996, to form the 14.10 special to Birmingham. *Brian Morrison*

46   LOST LIVERIES OF PRIVATISATION in colour

for the Modeller and Historian 47

Regional Railways North East (Northern Spirit / Trans-Pennine / Arriva Trains Northern / Northern Rail)

Left: The striking Northern Spirit livery of maroon with full-height diagonal capital 'N' in gold and 'transpennineexpress' in white and gold is well portrayed in this view of Class 158 No 158779 waiting to depart Manchester Piccadilly for Cleethorpes in June 2000.

Bottom left: In Northern Spirit livery, West Yorkshire PTE-owned Class 333 EMU No 333016 pauses at Skipton's Platform 3 while on a Bradford–Leeds working in May 2001. *Gavin Morrison*

Above: The hybrid Trans-Pennine scheme, half Northern Spirit and half FirstGroup, is shown on Class 158 No 158764 passing New Barnetby in September 2004 while *en route* from Cleethorpes to Manchester Airport.

Below: In Arriva colours of aquamarine and stone but devoid of any identification as to its operator (Arriva Trains Northern), Class 142 No 142021 makes its way out of Lincoln station, having disgorged its passengers after arriving from Huddersfield in September 2004.

for the Modeller and Historian

Above: In turquoise with full-height diagonal 'N' in green, Class 156 No 156475 comes to a halt at Haltwhistle (!) *en route* from Sunderland to Carlisle in August 2005. The livery anticipates the new franchise-holder, which has labelled the unit with a 'Northern' sticker.

Below: In an experimental Northern Rail livery of mauve, pale grey and white, Class 156 'Super Sprinter' No 156425 waits to leave Carlisle for Lancaster in August 2005. The trailing Class 153 is in North Western Trains blue with gold star.

50   LOST LIVERIES OF PRIVATISATION in colour

Above: Another experimental livery adorned Northern Rail Class 156 No 156451, also seen at Carlisle, in this case prior to departing for Newcastle in September 2006. *Brian Morrison*

Below: In standard Northern Rail colours but with pictorial vinyls promoting 'Yorkshire Working Together', Class 158 No 158787 leaves Selby in October 2007. *Ian Francis*

for the Modeller and Historian

51

ScotRail

Above: In the rather garish ScotRail livery of purple, white, pink and green, Class 170 DMU No 170404 makes ready to depart Kingussie on its way from Inverness to Glasgow in July 2003. *Ian Francis*

Left: The Strathclyde Passenger Transport colours applied to Class 334 EMU No 334025 stand out beneath the roof of Glasgow Central station as the unit waits to depart in June 2003. *Ian Francis*

Above right: In a rather more relaxed colour scheme than that applied to the Class 334s, Class 156 DMU No 156404 is seen at Carlisle in August 2005, having arrived on a service from Girvan. Much interest is being shown on the platform.

Right: The centre coach of Class 170 No 170415 was used to advertise *The Sunday Herald*, being seen thus at Aberdeen in May 2000. No 170414 was used similarly to promote daily paper *The Herald*, using grey as a base colour. *Brian Morrison*

for the Modeller and Historian 53

South Central (Connex SouthCentral / Southern)

Left: In temporary white (as worn for some time by quite a number of South Central units pending the application of Connex livery), Class 421 '4-CIG' unit No 1725 passes the site of Coulsdon North station in March 1997. The train, from Victoria, will be split into separate sections for Littlehampton and Portsmouth Harbour.

Below left: Standard Connex livery was white with a yellow lower bodyside band and a 'Connex South Central' inscription in blue. Thumping its way into Edenbridge Town in May 2000, Class 205 DEMU No 205018 is in no rush as it trundles from Oxted to Uckfield.

Bottom: To help passengers identify the First-class section some Connex South Central units were given a yellow roof band, and the number '1' alongside each cab window. Demonstrating these modifications is Class 421 '4-CIG' No 1907, leaving Havant on its way from Portsmouth Harbour to Victoria in June 1999.

Above right: Promoting a 'Good day out for everyone', a pair of Class 319s speed past Gatwick Airport non-stop on their way to Brighton in November 2000. The leading unit is No 319215.

Right: No 319004 was specially labelled to advertise the through Brighton/Gatwick–Rugby service operated by Connex. It is seen here leaving Kensington Olympia on just such a service to Brighton in August 2000.

Below right: Class 456 unit No 456006 was given a special livery, with standard GoVia Southern green cabs, promoting Transport for London Security. However, it ran for a few days prior to the application of its promotional vinyls, being seen thus passing Clapham Junction in February 2007 on an ECS working.

for the Modeller and Historian

55

South Eastern
(Connex SouthEastern)

Above: Connex SouthEastern's livery was was similar to that adopted by Connex South Central but with appropriate lettering and blue oval with white double CC logo on lower band in some cases. The Connex SouthEastern name and 'CC' logo are clearly visible here on Class 508 unit No 508203, pictured calling at Redhill whilst working a local service from Tonbridge to Three Bridges in December 1999.

Left: The blue solebar shows up well on ex-works Connex Class 423 '4-VEP' unit No 3493, seen having just passed beneath the footbridge west of Swanley Junction on its way from Ashford to Victoria in September 2003.

Above right: This classic view at Wandsworth Road features a pair of Class 365s, No 365502 leading, on their way from Victoria to Ramsgate in December 1997. This smart scheme was also applied to a few Class 465s.

Right: One South Eastern unit, Class 465 No 465214, carried advertising for Continental Airlines and is seen thus departing London Bridge for Sevenoaks on a service from Charing Cross in September 2004. The livery is quite different from the Continental scheme on Gatwick Express trains but similar to that applied to the Thameslink unit.

56   LOST LIVERIES OF PRIVATISATION in colour

for the Modeller and Historian

57

South Western (South West Trains)

Left: The earliest sign of privatisation – an orange stripe (below the red) added to standard Network SouthEast livery – is apparent on Class 442 No 2402 *County of Hants* as it passes Farlington Junction on a Portsmouth Harbour–Waterloo express in April 1996. The thin yellow stripe above the side windows indicates that First-class accommodation is in the leading carriage.

Below: A similarly modified version of NSE livery as applied to Class 455 units, comprising blue upper body, white lower bodyside with red and orange stripes upswept at the cab ends. The road bridge at the east end of St Margarets frames No 5736 as it heads towards the bridge over the River Thames near Richmond on a Hounslow loop service in March 2003.

Right: Whether this scheme can be classed as a lost livery of the privatised era is open to question, but it appeared after the critical date. Its repaint necessitated by a graffiti attack, Class 411 '4-CEP' No 1568 was given basic Network SouthEast livery minus the red band, being seen thus leaving Winchfield on a Southampton–Waterloo stopping service in November 1996.

Below right: The first repaints in South West Trains' current suburban red livery were turned out with a variation of the yellow area around the cabside. To celebrate the introduction of the new scheme in November 2004 a special train was operated from Waterloo to Hampton Court, Class 455s Nos 5711 and 5904 being seen here having just passed Wimbledon.

58

LOST LIVERIES OF PRIVATISATION in colour

for the Modeller and Historian

59

Left: No 5904 had earlier been one of four Class 455s selected to promote days out on South West Trains, being seen thus drawing into Berrylands station in April 2003 on its way from Hampton Court to Waterloo. The trees in the background have all since been cut down.

Below: Class 455 No 5864 was given a special 'Forget-Me-Not' livery to promote the charitable work of the Royal British Legion. It is pictured calling at Clapham Junction in May 2001 on what, despite its stated destination, was a Waterloo–Shepperton service.

Right: Along with a sister unit (No 5870) No 5864 was later given a revised Royal British Legion livery, with pink base colour shading to grey at the top. In August 2002 it was again photographed at Clapham Junction but this time heading in the opposite direction, having come up from Dorking.

Below right: Clapham Junction was always a good place to record the SWT advertising liveries, among them the excessive Legoland scheme applied to Class 455 No 5856. The unit is seen leading a train on a Kingston loop service in May 2005.

LOST LIVERIES OF PRIVATISATION in colour

for the Modeller and Historian

61

Above: Class 455 No 5853 shows off the Côtes du Rhône scheme as it approaches the up platform at Raynes Park on a service from Shepperton in April 2003.

Left: Another view at Clapham Junction, this time featuring the Golden Jubilee livery applied to Class 455 No 5868 and promoting locations including the Royal Botanic Gardens, Kew, and Hampton Court Palace. Photographed in September 2002, the train is bound for Strawberry Hill.

Below: Another photograph of No 5868, taken in August 2004 from the opposite end to show the Hampton Court Palace graphic. The location this time is Ashtead, the train a service from Dorking to Waterloo.

62 LOST LIVERIES OF PRIVATISATION in colour

Thames (Thames Trains)

Left: One of a number of units nationwide promoting London's Olympic bid, Thames Trains Class 165 No 165136 pauses at Bramley *en route* from Basingstoke to Reading in March 2005. A similar livery was applied to Great Eastern Class 315 No 315812 and Silverlink '313' No 313120.

Below: In a livery adapted (by the clever application of vinyls) from that of Network SouthEast, Thames Trains Class 166 unit No 166205 completes a classic scene at Little Bedwyn on its journey from Bedwyn to Paddington in August 2001. Note the sloping green door surrounds.

Bottom: Thames Trains livery as applied to Class 165 units, with oval green area around doors. The morning mist has lifted as No 165101 accelerates away from Mortimer on its journey from Basingstoke to Reading in April 2002. On the lower bodyside, the TT logo across a blue circle and red 'Express' was replaced after the franchise change by 'Link' with a logo and FirstGroup logo.

for the Modeller and Historian 63

Thameslink (Thameslink / First Capital Connect)

Left: A pre-privatisation picture of a non-standard pre-privatisation livery. In mid-grey with multi-coloured black and red patterns, Class 319 No 319035 arrives at Blackfriars on a service from West Hampstead to Sutton in July 1995.

Below: In standard Thameslink livery of dark blue with a yellow band outlined in white Class 319 No 319370 departs Sutton for Luton (not Bedford, as stated on the blind) in August 2004. Note the Metro 'M' logo on the cab-end door.

Right: Modified Thameslink livery, with yellow band replaced by white to suit First Capital Connect, on No 319378, seen working a Brighton–Bedford train near East Hyde in September 2006.

Below right: Showing off another modification to Thameslink livery, unit No 319440 stands at Harpenden station whilst working a Bedford–Brighton service in June 2005. The yellow window surround denoting First-class accommodation is much neater than various cantrail stripes used elsewhere.

64   LOST LIVERIES OF PRIVATISATION in colour

for the Modeller and Historian

65

Above: One unit was finished in plain blue with yellow doors. No 319010 is seen bringing up the rear of a Brighton–Bedford train leaving Gatwick Airport on a cloudy day in July 2006.

Left: Another one-off, in plain white with blue doors, was No 319001, seen leading a Brighton–Bedford train near East Hyde in September 2006.

Above right: Nos 319431 and 319456 were chosen to advertise Continental Airlines' services from Gatwick to New York and Houston. Its blue livery contrasting with the yellow and white of a Connex unit at the rear, No 319456 heads a Luton–Sutton stopping train calling at Harpenden in June 2005.

Right: Another unit selected to help promote London's Olympic bid, No 319422 shows off its mainly blue livery as it departs London Bridge *en route* from Bedford to Brighton in June 2005.

for the Modeller and Historian 67

Wales & West (Alphaline / Wessex Trains / Valley Lines)

Left: An early example of a temporary privatisation scheme is seen on Class 158 'Express' DMU No 158815, still in Regional Railways colours but with the addition of the Alphaline label. Photographed at Waterloo in October 1997, the train is waiting to depart for – of all places – Manchester Piccadilly!

Below: The full Alphaline scheme for Wessex services, with maroon doors, is seen on Class 158 No 158746 as it makes its way past the park at Millbrook while *en route* from Cardiff to Portsmouth Harbour in May 2002.

Right: Its blue doors identifying it as a Wales & West unit, No 158745 passes Dawlish Warren on its way from Bristol to Penzance in July 2000.

Below right: This experimental scheme for the Wessex operation was applied to one unit. Working a Cardiff–Portsmouth Harbour train, No 158867 is seen approaching Southampton Central in August 1999.

68   LOST LIVERIES OF PRIVATISATION in colour

for the Modeller and Historian

69

70　　　　　　　　　　　　　　　　　　　　　　　　　　　　　　　　　　　　　　　LOST LIVERIES OF PRIVATISATION in colour

Left: To match the Mk 2 stock used on Weymouth–Cardiff services Class 31/6 No 31601, hired from Fragonset Railways, was painted dark pink with 'wessextrains' in white. Recently named *The Mayor of Casterbridge* and with a bodyside label promoting the Heart of Wessex line, the locomotive is seen heading the Fridays-only Bristol–Brighton past Millbrook in July 2004.

Below left: The Class 150s were given a special livery promoting destinations served by Wessex Trains. Seen forming a Saturday Cardiff–Paignton service near Cogload Junction in July 2004 are Nos 150243 and 150247.

Above right: The Waterloo–Manchester service is featured once more, this time at Winchfield in July 2003, as Class 158 No 158842 shows off its *Western Mail* advertising scheme.

Right: By December 2005, when this photograph was taken, Arriva had taken over and had applied 'Times are Changing' livery to Class 158 No 158841, seen leaving Severn Tunnel Junction on a Gloucester–Swansea service.

Below: In a navy-blue livery promoting the city of Bristol, Class 143 No 143621 passes Undy on its way from Bath to Cardiff in September 2005.

for the Modeller and Historian

72   LOST LIVERIES OF PRIVATISATION in colour

Left: All the colours under the sun seem to feature on this train, seen passing Undy on a Saturday in September 2005 when Wales were playing at home. In a maroon-based livery promoting the Heart of Wessex line between Bristol and Weymouth, Class 153 No 153305 brings up the rear of a formation that also includes a similar unit extolling the virtues of Devon and Cornwall, one of the Class 150s in Wessex Trains promotional livery (as seen earlier on page 71) and, leading, a Class 158 in Wessex Alphaline colours.

Below left: Class 153 No 153320 was given this striking orange livery to promote Welsh tourism, being seen so adorned trundling past Undy in September 2005. Discernible on the side, along with Arriva's logo, is a quote from Dylan Thomas(1914-1953): 'And floating fields from the farm in the cup of the vales.'

Above right: Class 158 No 158821 shows off its Ginsters advertising livery as it leaves Lydney *en route* from Swansea to Birmingham in July 2003.

Right: Close-up of the cartoons that formed part of the Ginsters livery.

Below: A pair of Class 153s working a Southampton–Westbury service are seen passing Redbridge in March 2005. Promoting the 'great scenic railways of devon and cornwall' [*sic*], No 153374 is headed by a similar unit declaring its loyalty to the Heart of Wessex.

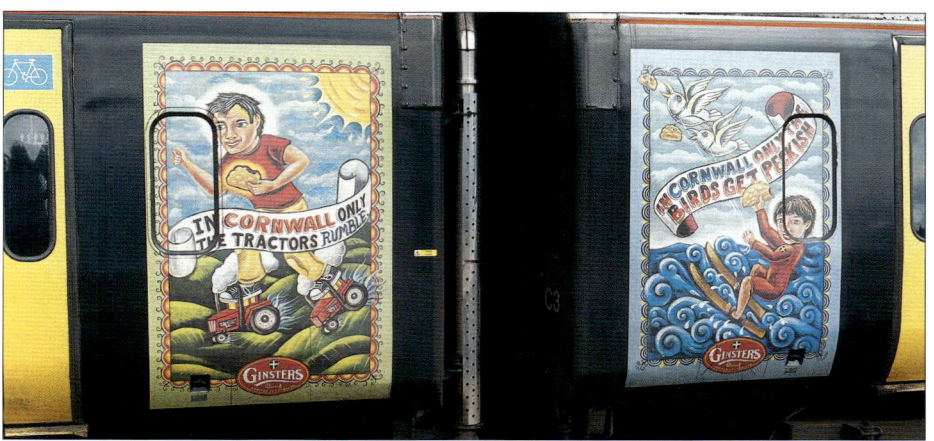

for the Modeller and Historian

73

Right: In 2004 Alphaline-liveried Class 158 No 158747 was decorated to celebrate the 200th anniversary of Richard Trevithick's pioneering steam-hauled train at the Pen-y-darren ironworks in South Wales. The unit is seen here passing Undy in September 2005 whilst working a service from Cardiff to Portsmouth Harbour.

Below: No 158855 had its standard Alphaline livery embellished with pictorial graphics encouraging visitors to 'Explore Exmoor'. Highlighted by low winter sun, it is seen passing Millbrook on a Portsmouth–Cardiff service in February 2007.

Bottom: In April 2005 No 158860 appeared in standard Alphaline livery but with pictorial graphics celebrating the 200th birthday of Isambard Kingdom Brunel. On its first day in service so adorned it was photographed passing Aller on a down working. *Colin J. Marsden*

74   LOST LIVERIES OF PRIVATISATION in colour

West Anglia Great Northern (WAGN / Stansted Express / ONE West Anglia / First Capital Connect)

Above: The first scheme for the WAGN Class 317s is shown to good advantage in this view of No 317657 pausing at Harlow Town on a Liverpool Street–Cambridge service in July 2004.

Left: A version of the original WAGN livery was applied to Hornsey depot's shunter, No 03179 *Clive*, seen newly painted for its commissioning in September 1998. Note the small triangular device and 'WAGN RAILWAY' logotype on the grey area just ahead of the cab. *Mick Barstow*

for the Modeller and Historian 75

Above: Caught by the sun at Bethnal Green in January 2002, No 315861 shows off its livery of deep purple with white doors and pink '**wagn**' logo. The train is a Liverpool Street–Chingford service.

Right: The Class 315s have appeared in a variety of liveries. In plain white with purple 'wagn' logo, No 315850 calls at Cheshunt *en route* from Hertford East to Liverpool Street in July 2004.

Below: In ONE livery with 'West Anglia' lettering, National Express having gained control of the franchise, Class 317 No 317672 awaits its next duty at Liverpool Street in July 2004.

76   LOST LIVERIES OF PRIVATISATION in colour

Right: Many Class 315s, along with some '313s', were given this promotional scheme, No 315844 being seen arriving at Bethnal Green on its way from Liverpool Street to Chingford in October 1999. The message daubed along the side reads: 'My Mum took me to London for £1 with a WAGN Family Travelcard'.

Below: Another Liverpool Street–Chingford service calls at Bethnal Green, this time in March 2004 and worked by Intalink-liveried Class 315 No 315857.

Bottom: Yet another Class 315 pictured at Bethnal Green *en route* to Chingford, No 315844 was one of two units (the other being No 315858) promoting Partners against Crime. Along with emergency telephone number 0800 40 50 40 it featured badges of participants in the scheme, including the Metropolitan Police and Tottenham Hotspur FC. This photograph was taken in May 2004.

for the Modeller and Historian

77

LOST LIVERIES OF PRIVATISATION in colour

Left: In a blue-based livery promoting the film *Harry Potter and the Philosopher's Stone*, Class 317 No 317670 is introduced to the public at King's Cross Platform 9¾ (in reality Platform 1) prior to departing for Cambridge in November 2001. *Brian Morrison*

Below left: One of four Class 365 units promoting destinations on the erstwhile WAGN network but served nowadays by First Capital Connect, No 365540 hurries through Brookmans Park on its way from King's Cross to Peterborough one Saturday in January 2008. The graphics on the side depict the Garden Cities of Hertfordshire. The other three units promoted Cambridge and Ely (No 365510), Peterborough (365519) and Norfolk (365531).

Above right: The Stansted Express units were used on a variety of workings apart from their designated duties. Seen at Carpenders Park in August 1998, Class 322 No 322483 is covering a Euston–Manchester Airport service on behalf of North West Trains; it would subsequently be repainted in NWT colours (see page 46).

Right: A number of Class 317s were refurbished for Stansted Express services and outshopped in a livery of iridescent blue, one such being No 317708, here passing Bethnal Green on a service from Liverpool Street in September 2000. The orange area discernible on the second carriage was intended to highlight access for the disabled.

Below: One of the Stansted Express Class 317s emerged in a simplified version of the 'one' livery, with appropriate lettering. Looking particularly smart, No 317729 is seen leaving Tottenham Hale on its way to Stansted Airport in July 2004.

for the Modeller and Historian 79

Above: Class 322 No 322485 was distinguished by its promotional livery for the Stansted Express services, being seen so adorned at Bethnal Green in October 1999.

Below: Advertising FinSpreads (and, on the other side, Mini CFDs), refurbished Class 317 No 317732 rushes through Harlow Town *en route* to Stansted Airport in July 2004. The decision to restrict advertising to just one coach of a four-car unit seems strange, especially when it presented such a contrast with the rest of the train, although it undoubtedly caught the eye.

NON-FRANCHISED PASSENGER OPERATIONS

Eurostar

Above: Thus far the Class 373 sets operated on Eurostar services have retained their original standard livery of grey, yellow and dark blue, but a number have been adorned with temporary promotional vinyls. Bringing up the rear of a Paris Nord–Waterloo express near Swanley Junction in July 2004, No 3001 displays a Disney advertising scheme.

Left: Adorned with multi-coloured vinyls publicising the re-release of the Beatles film *Yellow Submarine*, Nos 3005 and 3006 pass Wandsworth Road station on their way from Waterloo International to Paris Nord in September 1999. Neither this nor the previous picture can now be replicated, St Pancras having replaced Waterloo as the British terminus for Eurostar services. *Brian Morrison*

for the Modeller and Historian 81

Heathrow Express

Left: Unlike the majority of passenger-train services in Britain Heathrow Express is not franchised to a Train Operating Company (TOC), being provided instead by BAA. In a stylish livery of plain silver with black window surrounds, Siemens-built Class 332 No 332005 is seen in February 1998 waiting to leave Paddington on a test run to Heathrow Junction, where a temporary platform had been built pending completion of facilities at the airport.

Below: Contrasting with the elegant simplicity of the original Heathrow livery is this complex scheme applied subsequently to the driving coaches. Unit No 332012 leaves Paddington for Heathrow in August 2000.

Right: Vinyls adverting the Royal Bank of Scotland were applied to the Class 332 driving coaches. Here unit No 332007 forms part of a train leaving Paddington for Heathrow in January 2002.

Below right: A revised version of the Royal Bank of Scotland livery gave greater prominence to the company's initials. No 332012 is pictured on arrival at Paddington in November 2005.

for the Modeller and Historian

83

Hull Trains

Above: On its Class 170 DMUs open-access operator Hull Trains introduced a livery of dark turquoise and white, with a thin yellow band along the lower bodyside. No 170393 accelerates around the bend at Hornsey on its way from King's Cross to Hull in July 2004.

Below: In the later Hull Trains livery, 222102 speeds past Frinkley Crossing on its way from Hull to Kings Cross. August 2006.

CHARTER AND SPOT-HIRE OPERATORS

Cotswold Rail

Left: Class 87 No 87007 shows off spot-hire operator Cotswold Rail's original silver livery as it runs light past Carpenders Park in April 2006. Along with many others of its type this locomotive has since been exported to Bulgaria.

Below: For a while Cotswold Rail operated an HST set, and although the majority of the formation donned the company's silver livery one power car was outshopped in the colours of model-railway manufacturer Hornby. No 43087 is seen stabled at Stafford in March 2006. *Ian Francis*

for the Modeller and Historian

Fragonset Railways / FM Rail

Above: Spot-hire operator Fragonset Railways adopted a livery of black with a silver-edged red bodyside band and a silver roof, along with a traditional railway-style crest on one side of each cab. Looking for all the world like a 'OO'-gauge model, a Bedford–Bletchley stopping train comprising a pair of blue-and-grey Mk 2 carriages topped and tailed by immaculate Class 31/4s Nos 31452 and 31468 is seen near Lidlington in September 1998.

Left: Later Fragonset repaints were in unlined black with the company name prominent on the bodyside. Representing this style, Class 47/3 No 47355 *Avocet* passes Harrowden Junction at the rear of a special (headed by Class 45/1 No 45112) returning from Leicester to St Pancras in April 2004.

Below left: The only other locomotive with large Fragonset names, Class 73/1 electro-diesel No 73107 *Spitfire*, arrives at Bognor Regis in April 2006 with a special from Victoria. Note the cast Fragonset plaque on the cabside.

Above right: Fragonset Railways merged with charter operator Merlin Rail to form FM Rail, which retained black as the main colour but introduced a striking full-height bodyside logo in red, white and grey. The only locomotive to wear this livery was Class 47/4 No 47832, seen passing Denchworth at the rear of a 'Blue Pullman' working from Victoria to Lydney in October 2006.

Right: FM Rail's 'Blue Pullman' train, evoking memories of the bespoke high-speed diesel units of the 1960s, comprised a set of carriages painted in Nanking blue with white window surrounds (save on the restaurant cars) and a pair of matching Class 47/7s. Forming a charter train from Letchworth, the complete formation is seen taking the Portsmouth Direct line at Woking in January 2006, with No 47709 *Dionysos* leading and No 47712 *Artemis* bringing up the rear.

for the Modeller and Historian

87

Victa Westlink Rail / Stobart Rail

Above: Possibly the most repainted locomotive of recent times, Class 47/4 No 47832 is seen here in the striking livery of charter operator Victa Westlink Rail, which also had ambitions to run freight trains. The photograph was taken at Lower Basildon in July 2007. *Ian Francis*

Below: Victa Westlink's operations were curtailed when its parent company was bought out by the Stobart Group, an existing customer of freight operator DRS. In due course No 47832 was repainted in a blue livery, with stylised 'S' logos, for hauling the new 'Stobart Pullman', being seen passing through Liss Forest on its way back from Fareham to Victoria in May 2008. Alas the Pullman train would not attract the anticipated levels of custom, and No 47832 has now lost its Stobart decals, becoming a regular member of the DRS fleet.

LOST LIVERIES OF PRIVATISATION in colour

Waterman Railways

Above: An early proponent of privatisation was music impresario Pete Waterman, who acquired BR's charter unit, re-branding it as Waterman Railways and introducing a livery – lined black – resembling that of the erstwhile London & North Western Railway. On display at the Crewe Basford Hall open day in August 1995 (before the bulk of BR was privatised), Class 47/4 No 47488 *Davies the Ocean* makes a fine sight at the head of a train of Mk 2 carriage stock in LNWR 'plum and spilt milk'.

Below: In a different paint scheme Class 47 No 47707 *Guy Fawkes* passes Southampton with a Manchester–Bournemouth service in August 1999.

for the Modeller and Historian

89

FREIGHT OPERATORS

ARC

Right: The original ARC colours of yellow and grey were, in the eyes of the author, much more attractive than the later Hanson scheme. Here Class 59/1 No 59102 *Village of Chantry* takes the up main line at Bramshott with its Merehead–Woking stone train in March 1996.

Below: This revised version was worn for a short time by Class 59/1 No 59101 *Village of Whatley*, seen passing Berkeley Marsh in August 1998 with a rake of Yeoman hoppers *en route* from Theale to Merehead.

DRS

Above: Before Direct Rail Services' 'compass' livery (as applied from new to the company's Class 66 locomotives) became more widespread, older types wore this simpler version. Attached to the rear of a Grand Central driver-training special to Sunderland, Class 47/0 No 47237 leaves King's Cross in August 2007.

Below: Surplus to the requirements of Virgin Trains, a trio of Class 87s passed to DRS and were repainted blue. As it turned out they never entered service with the Carlisle-based operator, but in 2006, when the Royal Mail Class 325s were experiencing technical problems, they were used by GB Railfreight to power the Wembley Railnet–Shieldmuir parcels train. In May of that year, still in DRS blue but with the addition of orange surrounds to the cab windows and FirstGroup logo to the front, No 87022 passes Carpenders Park attached to the rear of the train while sister No 87028 does all the work.

for the Modeller and Historian

EWS

Above: Early repaints into EWS maroon and gold included an ampersand within the initials, clearly visible here on Class 73/1 No 73131 as it hauls NSE-liveried Class 421 '4-CIG' No 1704 through Surbiton on its way from Eastleigh to Stewarts Lane in March 1997.

Below: To avoid the cost of needless repainting, vinyl EWS decals, complete with the company's 'three heads' motif, have been applied to existing colour schemes. This is particularly true of the Class 92 electrics; here No 92034 *Kipling* brings the afternoon Wembley–Mossend freight past Carpenders Park in June 2006.

Above: The EWS decal blended in quite well with the Railfreight triple-grey, but its application to Mainline and Loadhaul colours was less successful visually. Making the point, Class 60 No 60044, still in Mainline blue, passes St Denys in March 2007 with a train of tank wagons on their way from Fawley to Newport.

Left: Another shade of blue applied to two Class 60s was this British Steel livery. Photographed in October 1997, No 60033 *Tees Steel Express* has arrived at Didcot from Avonmouth with a train of coal for the power station. The wording alongside the stylised 'S' logo reads 'Sections, Plates, Commercial Steels', while just discernible on the cabside is a metal EWS 'three heads' plaque.

Below: Matching the dignified colour of its train, EWS Class 37/4 No 37428 calls at Reading in June 1998 with a return 'Royal Scotsman' working bound for Paddington. Although this locomotive is still in maroon livery the details have been altered since this photograph was taken.

for the Modeller and Historian

93

Foster Yeoman / Mendip Rail

Left: A decade before the wholesale privatisation of BR, privately owned locomotives could be seen regularly in the form of the General Motors-built Class 59 diesels used on aggregates trains by Foster Yeoman. Pictured in its original livery, No 59003 *Yeoman Highlander* passes Sherrington with a train of empties on their way back to Merehead from Botley in May 1989.

Below: In 1993 the railway operations of Foster Yeoman and ARC were combined as Mendip Rail. The latter's very attractive colours are seen here in close-up as Foster Yeoman-owned Class 59 No 59002 *Alan J. Day* leaves the yard at Theale in May 2002 with empties returning to Merehead.

Right: No 59002 subsequently reverted to Foster Yeoman colours, albeit in a revised layout. Working the Hither Green–Whatley empties, the locomotive passes the site of Wolfhall Junction in April 2008.

Below right: In 2008 appeared a new Aggregate Industries livery, intended to be blue, green and silver, but on the first repaint the green appeared more like turquoise. Photographed before this was corrected, Class 59 No 59001 *Yeoman Enterprise* is seen at Eastleigh station in July 2008. *John Clark*

LOST LIVERIES OF PRIVATISATION in colour

for the Modeller and Historian

95

Freightliner

Above: In BR Railfreight triple grey but with red triangle motif and '**Freightliner**' in black alongside, Class 47/3 No 47361 *Wilton Endeavour* brings a Crewe–Grain Freightliner past the pylons at Hoo Junction in November 1999. This colour scheme was destined to be superseded on surviving older locomotives by a version of the green livery introduced with the company's first Class 66/5s.

Right and below: While in Freightliner ownership Class 47/4 No 47829 was painted to resemble a Police road vehicle, being seen thus at Millbrook Freightliner Terminal in August 2003 and subsequently passing Hanging Langford with a train of articulated Blue Circle Cement trailers bound for Westbury.

96   LOST LIVERIES OF PRIVATISATION in colour

GB Railfreight

Right: The original GB Railfreight livery of blue and orange with '**GBRf**' and the locomotive number in orange on the bodyside has been superseded on newer locomotives by FirstGroup house colours. Still in the original scheme, Class 66/7 No 66716 heads the Mountfield–West Burton Power Station gypsum around the sharp curve at Tonbridge in June 2004. At the rear of the train was No 66715.

Below: With large Union Jack applied to commemorate HM The Queen's Golden Jubilee, Class 66/7 No 66705 *Golden Jubilee* approaches Luton Airport Parkway on a Temple Mills–Croft working in November 2002. Note that the locomotive number now appears in small black numerals on the lower cabside.

National Power

Left: In 1996 National Power took delivery of its own fleet of six Class 59/2 locomotives, painted blue with red and white stripes and the company's circular logo midway along the bodyside. As yet unnamed, No 59206 heads an MGR train for Drax Power Station through the attractive station of Hensall in July 1996. National Power's Class 59 locomotives would subsequently pass to EWS.

for the Modeller and Historian

OTHER ORGANISATIONS

Adtranz

Left: In 1998 Adtranz unveiled a mock-up of a coach using a new body on an old frame (shades of the Southern Railway!) with the aim of enticing franchise-holders and the newly privatised rolling-stock companies (RoSCos) to invest in a cheaper form of rolling stock. Classed as a '424', the coach is seen on display at Victoria in May 1998.

Bombardier

Below: On loan to Midland Mainline, Bombardier Class 170 No 170397 leaves Luton Airport Parkway on a St Pancras–Derby service in November 2002. The 'Q jump' promotional livery makes a change from the standard fare.

Bottom: On loan from Bombardier to Central Trains but giving no clue as to either its owner or its operator, Class 170 No 170398 passes Gatcombe on its way from Cardiff to Nottingham in January 2004.

Hitachi

Above: To prepare for the introduction of its Class 395 'Javelin' units on high-speed domestic services in Kent, Hitachi had Class 310 EMU No 310109 converted as a 'Traction System Verification Train'. Now numbered 960201, it is seen inside Ilford depot on 9 December 2003. *Brian Morrison*

Hunslet Barclay

Below: In the early 1990s Hunslet Barclay was contracted to operate weed-killing trains on BR's behalf, motive power being provided by a fleet of six dedicated 20/9 locomotives painted in the company's livery of two-tone grey. Heading up the relief line at Potbridge (on the LSWR main line between Hook and Winchfield) in August 1992 are Nos 20901 *Nancy* and 20904 *Janis*. Note the white headcode discs.

Porterbrook

Left: As part of the process of railway privatisation Porterbrook Leasing ended up as the owner of numerous locomotives, but very few wore its own chosen livery of purple and white. Among those that did were a pair of Class 47/4s, Nos 47807 and 47817, of which the former, on hire to Virgin CrossCountry, is seen passing Coulsdon North at the head of a Brighton–Edinburgh express in September 1997.

Below left: A less predictable recipient of Porterbrook livery was 'Deltic' No 9016 *Gordon Highlander*, acquired by the company following a spell in preservation, but in this case the house colours were applied in a more sympathetic layout that reflected the locomotive's original scheme of two-tone green. Heading the Mid Hants Railway's 'green train', the locomotive is seen passing Sunningdale in December 2002 on a special working from Alton to Liverpool Street.

Bottom: A more 'contemporary' interpretation of Porterbrook livery was applied to the prototype Class 57/6 rebuild. Its bodyside number resembling graffiti, No 57601 speeds past Lower Basildon with a Paddington–Plymouth express while on loan to First Great Western in July 2001. Notwithstanding its appearance it clearly proved a success, FGW subsequently ordering four '57/6' conversions to an uprated specification.

Above right: Class 87 No 87002 was the only AC electric (thus far) to have been painted in Porterbrook livery and was further distinguished by having different styles applied on each side; the author's preference is for the version seen here as it propels a Liverpool–Euston express past Headstone Lane in June 2003. A nice clean locomotive, and the shadow of the mast has fallen between it and the coaching stock. Good luck? Of course not – photographer skill!

Right: Also at Headstone Lane, but this time in January 2005, No 87002 shows its other side whilst working to Birmingham 'wrong way round'; locomotives were usually to be found at the 'country' end.

100   LOST LIVERIES OF PRIVATISATION in colour

for the Modeller and Historian

101

102 LOST LIVERIES OF PRIVATISATION in colour

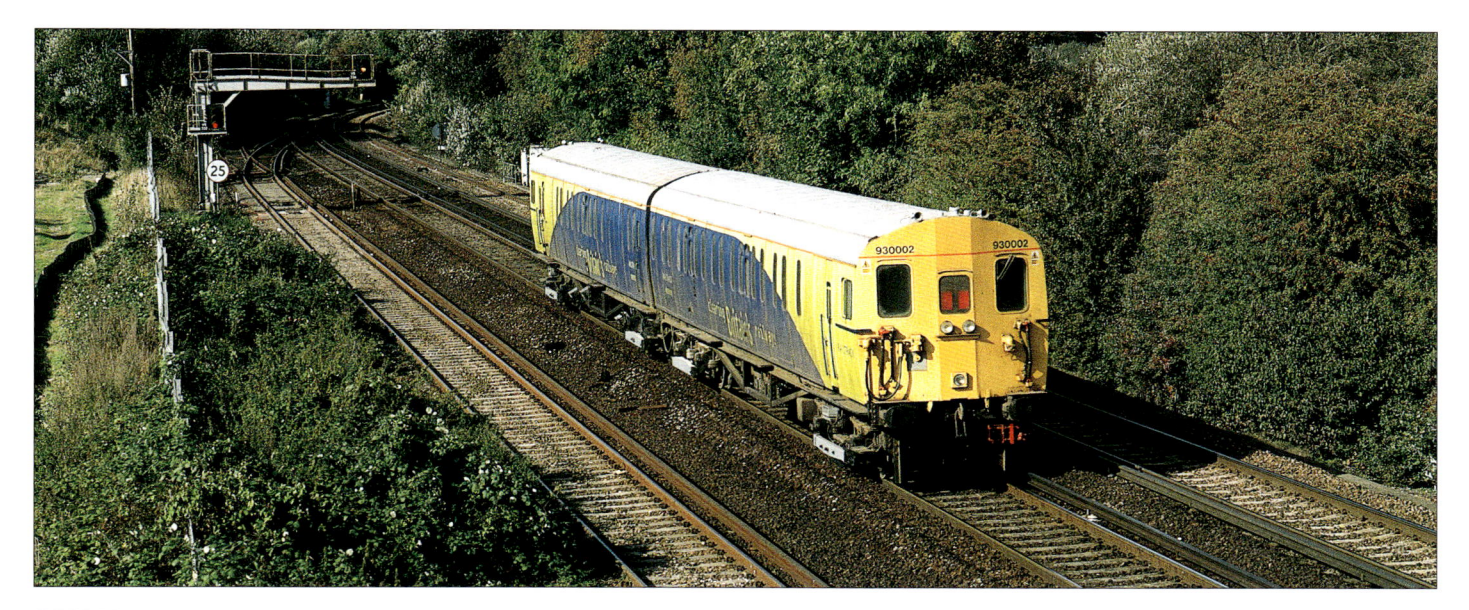

Railtrack

Above left: A view from the multi-storey car park by Eastleigh station in October 1996, featuring a Railtrack Class 930 heading north. The original colour scheme of light brown, white and grey shows up well in the autumn sunlight.

Left: A rare working on the DC lines at Headstone Lane as Railtrack Class 122 No 122019 trundles towards London in November 1999.

Top: Passing Otford Junction *en route* towards London in October 2002, Class 930 No 930002 shows off the later Railtrack livery of blue and lime green, with a silver roof. The legend on the side reads: 'clearing Britain's railways'.

Above: One Railtrack unit with a difference is No 960011, which is fitted with high-intensity lights to illuminate the track and check for defects. It is seen at Lower Basildon in May 2002.

Right: Further Railtrack activity at Lower Basildon, this time in December 2003, as Class 31/1 No 31190 *Gryphon* brings up the rear of a track-recording train headed by '31/6' No 31601.

for the Modeller and Historian

Above: An example of some of Railtrack's miscellaneous equipment, in this case a water-cannon unit, seen at Millbrook in August 1998. The variation in colours from those seen on page 102 is readily apparent.

Left: The short-lived, unsuccessful experiment of using MPVs for commercial purposes is represented by this photograph, taken at Moreton in August 2001, of Nos 98904 (nearer the camera) and 98906 (leading) transporting four containers from Willesden to Bulmer's at Hereford. Livery is the later Railtrack style, although on the MPVs very little of the lime green is apparent.

Wessex Traincare

Left: A visit to Eastleigh in June 1998 allowed the author the opportunity to record the rarely photographed Works shunter. Class 08 No 08649 (D3816) *G. H. Stratton* shows off its Wessex Traincare colours of grey and white with red and blue stripes; note also, on the cabside, the cast plaque depicting a Supermarine Spitfire fighter.

104   LOST LIVERIES OF PRIVATISATION in colour